Copyright © 2017 by Julie Rausch, JRPublishinggroup

All rights reserved.

No part of this book may be reproduced or distributed in any form without permission in writing from the author. Reviewers may quote brief passages in reviews.

CONTENTS

INTRODUCTION 1
CHAPTER ONE: WHY START AN ONLINE BUSINESS? 3
    MONEY 3
    FAMILY 4
    SELF-ESTEEM 4
    TAX BENEFITS 5
    SAVINGS 5
    FLEXIBILITY 5
    YOU ARE YOUR BOSS 6
    THINK OF IT AS AN INVESTMENT 6
    IT IS NOT EXPENSIVE 6
CHAPTER TWO: OVERCOMING ANY HURDLES 8
    STOCKING INVENTORY 8
    THE CAPITAL REQUIRED 8
    TECHNICAL ASPECTS 9
    BRAND REPUTATION 9
    SEO STRATEGY 9
    TARGET AUDIENCE 10
    PAYMENT GATEWAY 10
    CUSTOMER SERVICE 10
CHAPTER THREE: TARGET AUDIENCE 11
    YOUR BUSINESS PLAN 11
    RESEARCH, RESEARCH, AND RESEARCH 12
    DEVELOPING THE CUSTOMER PROFILE 12
    LOCATE YOUR AUDIENCE 13
    MONITOR AND EVOLVE 13
CHAPTER FOUR: BE AN EXPERT – BUILD A BRAND 14
    LOTS OF RESEARCH 14
    YOUR BRAND NEEDS A VOICE 15
    BALANCING YOUR MEDIA MIX 15

Web Business for Women

Live Your Dreams Making Money Online

By

Julie Rausch

Would you like more **FREE** tips and resources to help you achieve online success and wealth?

Please click the below link for my **FREE** offer:

"Easy Marketing Tips for Your Home-Based Business"

http://eepurl.com/c8rgw5

- SOCIAL MEDIA INTEGRATION 16
- BUILDING YOUR REPUTATION ONLINE 16

CHAPTER FIVE: SUCCESS MINDSET 17
- DEFINING SUCCESS 17
- SET GOALS FOR YOURSELF 17
- FIND SOME INSPIRATION 18
- CREATE HABITS THAT COMPLIMENT YOUR GOALS 18
- CREATE A ROUTINE BASED ON THOSE HABITS 18
- STOP PROCRASTINATING 19
- SUCCESS ISN'T THAT DISTANT 19

CHAPTER SIX: MARKET YOUR ONLINE BUSINESS 20
- SEARCH ENGINE OPTIMIZATION 20
- PAY-PER-CLICK ADVERTISING 21
- PUBLISHING AN E-NEWSLETTER 21
- START A BLOG 22
- SOCIAL MEDIA 22
- POSITIVE CUSTOMER REVIEWS 22
- OTHER TIPS 23

CHAPTER SEVEN: AFFILIATE MARKETING 25
- BUILD YOUR WEBSITE TRAFFIC FIRST, AND BE PATIENT 25
- ONE GOOD PRODUCT OR BUSINESS IS ENOUGH 26
- CONTENT IS VERY IMPORTANT 28
- PROMOTE YOUR SITE 30
- DON'T BE INVISIBLE OR ANONYMOUS 32

CHAPTER EIGHT: BLOGGING 34
- SETTING UP A BLOG 34
- USEFUL CONTENT 34
- FIND READERS 35
- BUILDING ENGAGEMENT 36
- START MAKING MONEY 37
- WHILE BLOGGING, KEEP THESE SIMPLE THINGS IN MIND. 39

CHAPTER NINE: VLOGGING 40

CHAPTER TEN: VIRTUAL ASSISTANT 44

- GENERAL OR ADMINISTRATIVE VIRTUAL ASSISTANTS 44
- DIGITAL MARKETING VIRTUAL ASSISTANTS 45
- PROGRAMMING VIRTUAL ASSISTANTS 45
- DESIGN VIRTUAL ASSISTANTS 45
- WRITING VIRTUAL ASSISTANTS 46
- A/V EDITING VIRTUAL ASSISTANTS 46
- FINANCIAL VIRTUAL ASSISTANTS 46

CHAPTER ELEVEN: FREELANCE WRITER/TRANSCRIBER 48
- STARTING A BLOG 48
- PITCHING A GUEST POST 48
- YOUR ALMA MATER 49
- WRITING A LISTICLE 49
- SELF-PUBLISHING A BOOK 50
- SIGNING UP FOR A CONTENT SITE 50
- BECOMING A COPYWRITER 50
- WRITING FAN-FICTION 51

CHAPTER TWELVE: AMAZON FBA 52
- WHAT IS FBA? 52
- WORKING WITH FBA 52
- FBA IN MOTION 53
- THINGS NEEDED 56

CHAPTER THIRTEEN: SELL YOUR KNOWLEDGE 57
- E-BOOK OR A WHITE PAPER 57
- A SEMINAR OR A CLASS 57
- TUTORING 58
- WRITING FOR WEBSITES 58
- CONSULTING SERVICES 59
- ANSWERING QUESTIONS 59

CHAPTER FOURTEEN: NICHE STORES ON EBAY, SHOPIFY 60
- FIND A NICHE 60
- SELECT A PRODUCT 61
- YOUR COMPETITION 61
- SETTING UP YOUR STORE 61

PRICING YOUR PRODUCT	62
COMPOSE PRODUCT PHOTOS	63
COMPOSE TITLES	64
CHAPTER FIFTEEN: DIRECT SALES - WHAT IT TAKES	66
COMPANY STRATEGY	67
A PRODUCT THAT EXCITES YOU	67
ATTITUDE MATTERS	68
GOOD AT NETWORKING	68
CONCLUSION	70

Introduction

I would like to thank you for purchasing this book, *'Web Business for Women - Live Your Dreams Making Money Online'* and I hope you find the book informative and interesting.

The Internet has managed to revolutionize all aspects of our lives, and the world of trade and commerce is no exception. You no longer need to be physically present to conduct your business. You can do so from the comfort of your own home! Web businesses are not only quite lucrative, but they also provide you the opportunity of doing something that you enjoy!

For years, I sat at a desk in a cubicle, working the daily nine-to-five grind in the insurance industry. I secretly dreamed of having my own business. I went back to school to become an aesthetician and did that for 14 years. I loved it because I was up and about, not tied to a desk, and meeting a lot of new people. Although I enjoy the aesthetics profession, I still longed for my own business, a business where I could be my boss and work from home or anywhere for that matter as long as I had my laptop. Through discovering my strengths and passions, and the explosion in Internet opportunity, my dreams of having my own business online came to fruition. And now I would like to encourage other women and share how to be successful with their own online business.

In this book, you will learn about web businesses, the benefits they offer, tips for creating the right attitude for becoming a successful entrepreneur, and the different ideas for starting your own business online. There are various options to choose from like content writing, blogging, affiliate marketing, FBA, vlogging, and so much more. You will find helpful tips and steps that you can follow for starting your own online business. So, are you ready to get started?

Chapter One:

Why Start an Online Business?

There is no time like the present to start your own business, and it has never been as easy as it is today. With the invention of social media and the advent of social media, you can connect with anyone regardless of their geographical location. Regardless of your social status, now you can share your skills and connect with people across the globe. If you are thinking about starting your own online business, it is quite economical and easy to get started. In fact, you can start your business for less than a $100 (yes, that's the cost of acquiring a domain name and a hosting service). If you can connect with your potential audience, you can indeed start your own business. There are plenty of benefits of starting your own online business. In this chapter, I have listed these benefits.

Money

Money is necessary, and it does make the world go around. We would all like to have some more of it though, wouldn't we? Whether it is for debt repayment, saving for retirement, or just for making ends meet, with the right knowledge, an online business can help you in earning money almost immediately. Unlike a conventional job, you needn't restrict yourself to just one avenue. You can select multiple avenues and work on all of them simultaneously. For instance, you can be a freelance writer, a blogger and an affiliate marketer! It depends on the time and effort you are willing to put into it.

Family

Let's be realistic now. If you are married and have children, then you will have your regular household chores to manage as well. It is not just your career, but your family that needs your time as well. A job that allows you to work from the convenience of your own home enables you to spend more time with your family!

Self-esteem

Most of us are so busy being mothers, wives and members of the community that we tend to forget that our lives are a reflection of our inner-selves. Starting your own business is a big accomplishment and something to be proud of; it will help in boosting your self-esteem and make you more confident as well.

Tax benefits

Most of the women who start an online business are doing it from their homes. They will be eligible for significant tax deductions for starting their home business. Fewer taxes mean more significant savings for you!

Savings

This is an obvious one. If you are working from home, then you don't have to splurge on expensive formal wear for your work. Women spend over $150 for an average professional suit! Can you imagine not having to buy expensive clothes for work anymore? Also, if you are working from home, you can conveniently cook your meals and brew your coffee. All these things might seem trivial but, over a period, you will be able to save a lot of money by not having to buy these things elsewhere.

Flexibility

You get to decide when and how you would like to work. There is no assigned workspace that you need to show up at. You can also work while you are traveling! All you need is your laptop and a good Internet connection, and you are good to go! This also means that you can spend more time with your loved ones. You can take a day off whenever you feel like it. You have the power to decide how much work you are willing to take on and the amount you want to make. You no longer have to worry about being paid less than your actual worth, and you don't have to ask anyone for a raise. With the right knowledge, persistence and hard work, you can generate as much income as you want to.

You are your boss

You don't have to worry about layoffs. Who will fire you, when you are your boss? You have the power to make all the decisions. This doesn't mean that there aren't any risks, but you can at least control what you are doing, and you aren't at someone else's mercy anymore.

Think of it as an investment

If you manage to build a successful online business for yourself, you can always sell it in the future and profit off of your hard work.

It is not expensive

As I mentioned earlier, numerous small businesses started building their business empires with just a domain name and a hosting service for housing their business website.

Start an online business, because you want to do something for yourself and not because of what someone else says.

Chapter Two:
Overcoming Any Hurdles

There are a couple of hurdles that you might face while starting a web business of your own. In this chapter, you will learn about these hurdles and how you can turn them in your favor.

Stocking inventory

It is important to keep stock of your inventory if you have an online store. A little extra inventory is helpful but too much of it might go to waste, and it will just increase your expenses. Before you can think about becoming an online seller, you must research the niche you are catering to and understand the demand for the product you are thinking about selling. When you have these metrics at hand, you can maintain your inventory levels accordingly.

The capital required

Regardless of the business you are thinking about starting, capital is required. Capital is the initial investment you will need to make for starting your own business. You don't need to invest a lot in starting your web business. However, remember that profits might not be instantaneous, and you will need to prepare yourself financially. Research and analyze the market before taking the plunge.

Technical aspects

If you are a web or a graphic designer, then you are certainly equipped to design your website. However, if you have no idea about designs, then you should hire some help for doing so. You don't have to do everything by yourself. You might do more harm than good to your business if you aren't sure of the technical aspects involved in starting a web business.

Brand reputation

This is perhaps one of the biggest fears an e-commerce business owner could harbor. Make use of social media for engaging with your customers. The more you engage and the more attention you pay to what they like and dislike, the better your chances of improving your reputation.

SEO strategy

As and when your website, vlog, or blog is ready, you need to have a good SEO or digital marketing strategy in place. SEO helps in improving your online visibility, and this is extremely important for an online business.

Target audience

Who is your target audience? Do plenty of research to understand the market you are targeting and the demand for the product or service that you are offering. If there is no demand for what you are offering, then the chances of your success are going to be quite low.

Payment gateway

There are multiple payment options to choose from, and as a business owner, you are supposed to select a payment gateway that your target audience is comfortable with. You can opt for wire transfers, PayPal, credit or debit cards, and so on.

Customer service

Providing good customer service is essential for any business. If a customer is satisfied with the service you provide, it is likely that they will come back. If they aren't, then the chances of bad publicity tend to increase as well. Keep collecting feedback and make the required changes for improving your customer service.

Chapter Three:
Target Audience

If you were just starting your business, then you would have spent a lot of time planning and building it. A significant part of this process is deciding who will be on the receiving end of all the efforts you are making. The product or service you are offering is as important as the target audience. As a business owner, you will want to have as many customers as possible. In this chapter, you will learn about finding your target audience.

Your business plan

Start by taking a look at the goals you have set for yourself and carefully analyze the products or services that you are offering. Think about the need or the problem that your products or services will help in fulfilling or solving. Also, think about the defining factor that will differentiate your business from that of your competitors. Think about the information you require and the need for the same. What do you need to know about your target audience for reaching them? Consult your business plan and decide who your target audience is. Don't think about the people you would want to sell to. Instead, think about all those who are looking for the product or the service that you are offering.

Research, research, and research

Secondary research is important. There are plenty of sources that you can gather information from about the industry, niche, competitors, and target audience that you are looking at. Secondary research involves using information that someone else has already gathered and you don't have to do all the research again. However, don't depend on it entirely. Do some research of your own as well.

Developing the customer profile

Once you have completed your research, you must create a customer profile. This is so much more than just a simple statement. It is a detailed description of who your likely customers will be and include certain demographic and psychographic information about them. It can involve data about the potential customer's age, gender, location, income, and other demographic information and psychographic information like hobbies, interests, attitudes, and so on. This information is quintessential for developing your customer profile. Demographic information will help you in identifying who your customer is, and psychographic information assists in determining why the customer needs your product or service.

Locate your audience

Your work doesn't stop after identifying your target audience. You need to find the websites and social media networks they frequently use. Get involved and form a presence for yourself by posting on these websites and social media sites. Do they like checking their emails or is there a particular app that they love to use? Make use of all this information and combine it with the customer profile, and you can locate your customers.

Monitor and evolve

Once you have identified your target audience, you will need to keep researching continuously for understanding the current market trends and your competition in the industry. Keep track of how your customer is evolving. Before you start marketing, you need to know how you plan on tracking the sales, interactions, requests for information, and other data.

Chapter Four:
Be an Expert – Build a Brand

Investing in your brand online is a crucial step since it allows you to create an entity that will resonate with your customers and keep them coming back for more. Building your brand online will help you in improving the awareness and reputation of your brand. The more people that are invested in your brand; the greater are the chances of your customers staying loyal. If you are interested in the growth of your online business, you will need to work on the growth of your brand. Here are five things that you should keep in mind if you are interested in building your brand on the Internet.

Lots of research

The first step in building your brand is to have a thorough understanding of your target audience, especially before you start creating strategies for content and communication. There are plenty of online tools that you can make use of for identifying your target audience. Make use of the information provided it the previous chapter to identify your target audience.

Your brand needs a voice

Depending on the research, you can determine what your audience would want to her and the message you would want to put forth. This will help in establishing the foundation for your brand. While you are doing this, you will need to keep a couple of things in mind. Always keep an open mind and consider all the ideas that before selecting one. While creating and developing content, you should speak with your audience and check the topics that they can relate to and the information that keeps them engaged.

Balancing your media mix

You should make use of different channels for building your brand. Make use of content and display networks to publicize about your brand through repletion and make use of behavioral marketing for targeting your audience. From the perspective of organic search, your brand name and message should be consistent with the title tags and Meta descriptions you use. Your message should be in perfect harmony with your brand's voice. Consistency is key to improving your brand's visibility.

Social media integration

What are the kind of interactions you would want your customers to have with your business? What would you want your brand to convey on social media? What is the right social media platform for you? You might not have all the answers right away, but with a little research, you will be able to understand where your audience is located and how you can improve your interaction with them.

Building your reputation online

It is quite similar to networking, but it does take some time and effort. You will need to have a well-defined strategy that you can make use of to reach out to your target audience. The next step is to identify all the different tactics that you can use. For instance, you can leverage any of the existing offline partnerships that you might have for growing your online reputation.

Chapter Five:

Success Mindset

Having the right attitude matters as much as the work that you are doing, if you want to achieve success. In this chapter, you will learn about the seven steps that you can follow for achieving success from the inside out.

Defining success

If you don't define what success means to you, then you will keep subjecting yourself to confusion about what is a success and what is a failure. Think about what is important to you in your personal and professional lives. Take a while, set your ego and guilt aside, and think what your idea of a "perfect life" is.

Set goals for yourself

Now that you know what success personally means to you, you need a plan for achieving that success. Without a plan or a strategy, you will never be successful. So, you must start setting goals for yourself.

Find some inspiration

Setting goals does not serve any purpose if you don't convince your brain to stick to those goals. Look for something that inspires you and motivates you. You can read inspirational books, watch motivational videos, or visualize what you would feel after achieving your goals. Really get in touch with those good feelings that would follow manifestation of your dreams and goals. These things will keep you going, even when things seem impossible and tough.

Create habits that compliment your goals

Setting goals work well when you develop habits surrounding those goals. There is a direct relationship that exists between your goals and the rate of depletion of motivation. If you aren't habitual in doing things for achieving your goals, then your motivational levels are bound to plummet.

Create a routine based on those habits

Successful people know how to live their success, regardless of whether others notice it or not. You must learn to live your success. Always put your best foot forward and do the best you can. Tackle all the tough tasks that come your way and don't give up.

Stop procrastinating

Routines are essential and not having one will lead to wastage of time and effort. There will be times when you will feel dejected and feel like nothing is working in your favor. Or there might be times when you don't feel like doing something, and everything seems pointless. In such cases, you need to stop procrastinating and get on with your work. Take a break if you feel like it, but don't postpone your work.

Success isn't that distant

Stop thinking that success is a distant achievement. It is as distant as you perceive it to be. Stop wishing for success and start doing things that will help you in achieving the success you have been dreaming of!

Chapter Six:
Market Your Online Business

Having a website alone doesn't do the trick anymore. If you want to increase your rate of success, then you need to learn about marketing your business online. In this chapter, you will learn about different things you can do for increasing the visibility of your website, generating more traffic, and increasing your sales.

Search engine optimization

The basis of SEO is to write the website copy in such a manner that your website will appear high on the result pages of popular search engines when a user uses a specific keyword for searching. You can make use of the services offered by different companies for optimizing your site. Well, you can try your hand at SEO if you want to. Think of a couple of simple words or phrases that a customer might make use of while searching for a business similar to yours, and then type it into any of the popular search engines like Google or Bing. You will receive results for similar phrases that were searched. Pick a longer phrase and a couple of keywords, and use them in the copy of your website's home page.

Pay-per-click advertising

SEO and Pay-per-click are often clubbed together as a tool for increasing the traffic to a given website. However, these two aren't similar and are quite different. When it comes to PPC, you can purchase a couple of keywords and phrases from a search engine based on pay-per-click. For instance, let us assume that you are selling skateboards in a particular city. If you purchase the keyword phrase "skateboards in _____ city," an ad for your website will appear in the "paid results" section of the search. Whenever someone clicks on such a link, they would be redirected to your website, and you will need to pay a pre-decided fee to the search engine.

Publishing an e-newsletter

You can drive traffic to your website by publishing e-newsletters. When this is done properly, it will enable you to reach your target audience consistently and direct them to your website for more information about your business, the products or services offered, and so on. The secret to publishing a good e-newsletter is to develop a database carefully and to provide some valuable content to the target audience instead of a poorly veiled sales pitch. Also, the recipients should have the option of opting out of the newsletter whenever they want to.

Start a blog

You can improve the rankings of your website by writing a blog. Write a blog and post the links to your website in it. This will help in diverting some traffic to your website. You can use the same keywords and keyword phrases in your blog as you did for your website.

Social media

Social media platforms are primarily meant for socializing. However, their function isn't just limited to that. You can make use of social media to promote and market your business online. This is the best manner in which you can connect with your target audience. You can make use of social media to divert web traffic to your website as well. You can start a Facebook page or group and do Facebook Ads to gain members.

Positive customer reviews

Whenever you buy something online, do you look at the reviews that a particular seller has received? Would you be comfortable while buying products from a seller on Amazon with two stars or with four stars? You would obviously choose a seller with positive customer reviews. Not just that, there are plenty of websites that help in posting reviews online. Make sure that you reply positively to a comment posted by a customer regardless of whether it is positive or not.

Other tips

Even if the idea of getting started with online marketing seems daunting, do not panic. It might seem tricky, but it is simple. You have already done the most difficult thing: leaping into an unknown territory by starting your own business! Kudos on that and don't lose your nerve now! Don't expect any immediate results. Spend some time and create an online marketing strategy that can work in your favor. You just need to spend about 2 to 4 hours every week doing this. You can start by acquiring a URL for your web business. There are plenty of services to choose from and buy an online name that is suitable for your business. You can always personalize it in some form. Once you have a URL, the next step is to decide on the kind of technology you are inclined towards. You can make use of a conventional website or a blog-style website. Wix.com, Godaddy.com, and Wordpress.com are excellent sites for beginners. You will need to set up a storefront for your web business. It doesn't have to be anything jazzy; you can try the minimalistic route instead.

Like I already mentioned, don't underestimate the power of keywords and keyword phrases. This is the best way to direct web traffic to your website. The reviews your business receives needn't always be favorable. At times, you can receive unfavorable reviews as well. When this happens, make sure that you handle it professionally and don't let your emotions dictate an answer. Make the most of social media and create social media presence for your web business! Also, remember that you don't have to do everything on your own. It is okay to ask for help. If you feel that you need help with any aspect of starting and running a business, join entrepreneurial groups on Facebook or groups that are similar to your niche, or seek mentors and professional help.

Chapter Seven:
Affiliate Marketing

One of the easiest ways in which you can make money online is by taking up affiliate marketing. You don't have to work on product ideas, product creation, providing customer support, or any other problems that are associated with the creation and development of a product. All that you need to do is just promote a product.

Build your website traffic first, and be patient

Affiliate marketing thrives on people's interest in clicking on links to products that catch their eye. But who are these "people"? All those who visit your blog or website to read what you have written. So, make your blog or site as interesting as possible, if you are interested in luring them. Remember that you need to establish a good reader base to land an affiliate marketing gig. Your content should be as engaging as the look of your blog or website.

If you're not getting a good number of unique to your website, you're not going to get the click-through to your affiliate. Here, "unique" refers to new customers and not the same old ones who have probably bookmarked and keep visiting all the time. The traffic to your blog or site increases when the number of people visiting it is going to increase. Not everyone is going to click on the links, and to get a reasonable number of clicks; you need plenty of regular visitors. You also need to build up a reputation as an expert in your niche before people trust you enough to go for your recommendations. There should be interesting content for people to read and remain glued. It is not helpful if they visit just once and immediately forget about your blog. You need to track the number of people that visit your page and record the numbers per day, month and year. This will help you in knowing how popular your blog is.

One good product or business is enough

Now that we understood who these "people" are, it will help you in generating good traffic come your way, let us look at what they will be interested in.

Newcomers to the system often make the mistake of peppering their site or sites with lots of different things, imagining that people are likely to buy more because they have more choices. It is typical human thinking to want a lot of choices in anything and everything, let alone links on a website. You are not a store – you don't have to offer your customers choices because they did not land on your site with purchase in mind. They're there for information, and if you're good at what you do, you'll be able to persuade them to buy something while they are there so that you can make some cash.

Think of it as a classy gig to have only one website promotion, and that website is the best one that your readers can have. That is, you will have the chance to promote one product or service better rather than having to do it for five or six different ones. Not only will that confuse your customers but will confuse you as well. You will have to look into two or three different companies and think of where their links will look the best. Think of yourself as a pop-up store to promote one product as opposed to a supermarket that offers a lot of choices.

The power of suggestion works for a majority of the customers. They will take a liking to something if you tell them that you are offering them the same product that you have personally tested and liked yourself.

Don't make the mistake of putting up too many choices at once. If you have put up just one product and the website is offering it at the best price in the market then even if the person has left your site to do a quick price comparison, he or she is sure to return to yours to click on the ad. Also, focusing on a single product or business makes it easier to make keywords work for you. So, stick with one business or product. If you want to do more, set up a different website for each affiliate, and concentrate on that, rather than spreading yourself too thin. What you can then do is, try and link your sites.

Content is very important

This is true of any website of course, but it's especially relevant if you are hoping to make money from affiliate marketing. People go to websites to be informed or entertained – often both at the same time. So, make sure you have plenty of content structured around the products or business you are promoting.

Another point to remember is that search engines can tell whether there's quality content on your site, and will rank it higher as a result. That means more visitors and hopefully more sales. You must be well versed in the concept of "SEO." SEO refers to search engine optimization. You must have heard that many companies have a good SEO team which helps them in becoming popular. Well, this is true because these teams will work hard on promoting the websites and blogs of the company and help it appear on top of the Google search list.

You should pick out all the top words from your blog or website, which are most likely going to be typed by people. If they get the combination of words right, then your site is going to appear as the topmost links. For this, you can also make use of a small description that will help you put in all the main words.

But remember just a good SEO description will not do the trick, and you need to have a good content as well. So, forget about the keyword-stuffed sales pitches when you are coming up with the content for your blog – educate, inform, entertain, but whatever you do, don't spam. You don't need long articles – in fact, three hundred-word posts will hold the attention of your audience better than one 800 to 900-word post. The more information you give away, the better the reader base. Most people will look for sites that will give them an in-depth look at difficult topics. By making it easy for them, you will have a chance to increase your reader base.

You need to be as different and unique as possible. For instance, if you wish to provide customers with recipe ideas then come up with good and unique ones that are not easily available on the Internet. Once they take a liking to your unique recipes, they will be interested in clicking on an ad on your site, which might be a particular cream cheese brand or even baking trays. You can also explicitly mention that you have used these brands and hyperlink the products with the words. Your readers are sure to click on them!

Keep the posts on the topic, and plant the idea in the reader's mind that they need to buy whatever you're promoting. You can even drop a contextual link to a particular product in the content. Help them reach a decision, rather than trying to direct them straight to the sales site. The soft approach is the best approach here as you are trying to be subtle about your promoting. I am sure you have bought many things by clicking on ads put up on blogs and sites that you read.

Promote your site

This sounds obvious, but if you want people to come to your site, read your content and click on your affiliate links, you need to let them know the site exists. Whether it is a product or a service, everything needs to be promoted for people to be aware of what you are doing. Without proper promotion, how are people going to get word about your website out there? There are only so many friends that will click on your links and for you to land a big gig; you will need at least 1000 clicks a week.

Firstly, list your site in search engines, write press releases to be distributed online, and promote your site on forums in your niche and social media.

If you have a friend whose blog is extremely popular, then you can consider asking him or her to subtly promote yours on theirs. But you might have to consider paying them a small fee for it, as you will be benefitting from their service to you. If you don't have any such friends but know of someone who has such a blog, then you can consider contacting them and asking them politely to promote yours. It's a good idea to have Facebook and Twitter account linked to your website and set up so that each time you post an update on the site, it's posted to your social media account. You can also have a Facebook page dedicated to your website or blog where you will keep updating with links to your site. Work on building an army of followers, but don't even consider buying them. Bought followers are not going to go to your website and click on the affiliate links – they just give an illusion that your social media account is more popular than it is. You might think of being popular but once the bubble bursts, you might be extremely disappointed. If it is a group of friends, then make sure the group is genuinely interested in your blog or site and are not just doing you a favor. Those will only last for a while and decide to abandon you once they lose interest.

Don't be invisible or anonymous

This is a golden rule. First and foremost, you must have confidence in who you are and what you do. If you don't have self-confidence, then it will not work in your favor. Just because it's easy to hide behind an alias on the Internet, it doesn't mean you should. It can be tempting to use a cool name but don't do so. If you want to build credibility and earn money online, you have to be seen as a real person, with proper contact details. Don't hide behind a pen name or a nickname, use a real name and an email address tied to your domain name, rather than a Hotmail or an AOL account. If you wish to use a pen name, then consider putting it in brackets so that the person is aware of your real name as well. Make sure you write out your full name including initials, as there can be many others with the same name as you. Remember that people need to know they can contact you with questions and that they will get an answer from a real person. They might also ask for a genuine photograph just to be sure of who the other person is. If they can't trust the Webmaster, they're not going to click on the affiliate link, and you won't make any money. It's all about trustworthiness.

Before you start to make money from affiliate marketing, you need to have your site set up to encourage people to click through on the advertising links. That means having great content that's informative and entertaining, earning a reputation for being an expert in your niche and taking a soft approach to selling. Let your knowledge and enthusiasm persuade the reader to click through, rather than filling the site with banners and sales pitch. Also, be sure to provide proper contact details, so your readers know you are a real person.

Chapter Eight:
Blogging

In this chapter, you will learn about making money by becoming a blogger! Blogging is fun if you like writing and sharing on social media. Here is how to make money from a blog.

Setting up a blog

Well, this one is pretty obvious, isn't it? You cannot possibly make money by becoming a blogger if you don't have a blog! Blogging is simple, and you don't have to feel intimidated or overwhelmed at the thought of creating your blog. You can start by creating your blog on WordPress if you want to.

Useful content

You cannot have a successful blog without posting any useful content. Your primary focus should be on churning out content that others would want to read about. Take some time and select a topic. Once you have done this, you can start writing about it. The key to becoming a successful blogger is by catering to the needs of a niche or a particular demographic. The content that you create should be useful to your audience. It doesn't have to change their lives necessarily, but it certainly should add some value!

Find readers

Once you have started writing and creating useful content, you should start focusing on building your reader base. Most of the bloggers tend to have a "build it, and readers will automatically come to" mentality, but this is nothing but a trap. If you are interested in making money from your blog, then your focus shouldn't be just on building a great blog, but also on having a good number of followers as well. So, you need to get off the blog and start promoting your blog! There are different ways in which you can experiment with increasing your blog's audience. You need to be able to divert and retain traffic that comes to your blog. The first step is to think about the kind of readers you would like to have read your blog. You can create a reader profile, and this will help in attracting the kind of audience that you are looking for. Once you know the kind of audience you want, you can start looking for places where such audience would gather. Start by listing down answers to these questions:

- Are they reading any specific blogs? Make a note of the top 3 blogs.

- Are they participating in any forums? Make a note of the top 3 forums.
- The social networking platforms they are active on? Make a note of the top 3 social networking media for this purpose.
- Are they listening to any podcasts? If yes, then list the top 3 podcasts.

These are great places for attracting the kind of readers that you want. Now that you are aware of where to find your target audience, you need to make the most of these platforms and make your presence felt. Keep building awareness about your blog and increase your audience base.

Building engagement

When you start focusing on creating good and useful content and finding readers for your blog, you will start noticing that people are not just visiting your blog, but they are engaging with the content of it as well. When this starts happening, you will need to concentrate on engaging with your audience as well and building yourself a community of readers and followers. Respond to all the comments that they post and keep them engaged. Keep them coming back for more.

Start making money

Once you have started your blog, created good content, found readers, and have started engaging with them, the next step is to start making money from your blog. Monetizing your blog is not an easy feat, and you will need to put in a lot of effort. Here are different income streams that you can consider making money from.

- Advertising: This is where most of the bloggers usually start. This is similar to the advertisements that you would find in magazines and newspapers. Once the web traffic to your blog starts growing, you can find advertisers who would be willing to pay you a fee to gain access to your followers. You will need to have decent traffic if you want to truly capitalize on this.

- Affiliate marketing: You can start earning by taking up some affiliate marketing on your blog. You simply have to post the affiliate links to specific products listed on a particular website. For instance, you have started a blog about baking recipes; you can perhaps post a link to a gourmet online store that you keep acquiring your produce from. By doing this, you will earn a commission on a sale that is made whenever a buyer clicks on the affiliate link.

- Events: This isn't something that a lot of bloggers tend to do, but it is quite lucrative as well. You can host an event and earn some money. You can host online or offline events, depending on your convenience. You can charge your readers for entering the contest or the event, or you can find a sponsor for the event. Online events have become quite popular these days.

- Recurring income: An increasing number of bloggers are opting for recurring income streams these days like membership or continuity programs. This is when the readers are required to pay a recurring fee to access premium content, some specific service, or online tools being offered on the blog.

- Promoting a business: You can start promoting regular brick-and-mortar businesses on your blogs. The businesses would pay you a fee for accessing your reader base.

- Services: You can also start offering different services to your readers like coaching, consulting, copywriting, training, designing, and much more.

While blogging, keep these simple things in mind.

You cannot post links directly on your blog. You will have to direct your users towards a homepage where the necessary content is present or the brand's website description that has a clickable link to it. A picture is indeed worth a thousand words. However, a collage that consists of 44 images isn't worth 4000 words. If you want to market your brand or business successfully, then make sure that the images you are posting are clear, identifiable, and large. Keep things simple. Make sure that you are posting actively and according to the engagement pattern of your followers. When it seems that they are most likely to engage, that's when you should post. This will take a while to get it right and spend some time trying to figure this out. It might not sound important, but it most certainly is. Keywords are quite important. Keywords help the users in discovering your content. Be judicious in your use of keywords and keyword phrases. Always remember to respond to any direct comments, opinions, and questions.

Chapter Nine: Vlogging

Vlogging refers to video blogging and in this vloggers share their ideas, thoughts, routines, snippets from their daily life and much more. A vlogger documents their daily life and shares the same on the Internet. This is done to gain the attention of the audience and to keep them engaged.

Here are a couple of things that you would need as a vlogger if you were interested in making money from vlogs.

The number of opportunities that come along your way will increase with an increase in the viewers your vlog receives. One of the most popular platforms for vlogging is YouTube. If you have a YouTube channel with a significant number of followers, then the number of opportunities you have will increase as well. You should be consistent with the way you upload your vlogs and engage with your viewers; growth is bound to happen. When you are consistent, people will automatically start liking and commenting on the vlogs you post. The greater the number of subscribers and followers you have, the higher are your chances of landing promotional gigs.

The cinematography does make a difference in profiting with vlogging. Essentially vlogging is about being innovative and being genuine on the camera. Notwithstanding that, what attracts a lot of people is great quality video. An excellent quality video implies your recordings must be splendidly shot, cinematography ought to be innovative, and the substance being shared is significant.

The narrating is likely the most critical piece of the vlog. If you want to get your audience hooked on to what you are offering, then the narrative needs to be engaging. It reflects in your entire vlog. It's something that associates a considerable measure of things together, for example, vlog story + vlog title + vlog thumbnail + vlog content. Each vlogger has an alternate method of recounting the story. Some of them have long and loquacious vlogs. They share their day to day life minutes while doing day by day routine errands, spending some time with their family while cooking, feasting at the lodging, and now and then shopping with family.

One of the essential things is an incredible thought process. It relies on the vlogger. What you are sharing should be a reflection of who you are. Vlogging is about inventiveness and also innovativeness. Try not to constrain yourself to a couple of thoughts that somebody tells you for profiting from vlogging. Continue researching and finding new ways to serve your crowd when you get started. After this point, consider benefiting because toward the day's end, any individual who ever profits with vlogging is somebody who began vlogging for enthusiasm and not to profit out of it.

You can just begin profiting with vlogging by joining the YouTube partner program. This is the least complex approach to begin. Ensure your record is in a great standing. Go to your dashboard and search for the adaptation tab to initiate it and follow simple steps to get started. When it's set, it may take a couple of days to get the endorsement, but once that is done, you'll be ready. From that point on, you'll be profiting off of your recordings.

Take up vlogging only if you are fascinated and passionate about it. You cannot fake enthusiasm, and you indeed cannot hold an audience if you don't like what you are doing. You can make use of your vlog to promote any particular product if you want to. If you have developed an affiliate marketing or selling the program for yourself, then you can certainly make use of your vlog for promoting the same. If you can hold onto your viewers and keep increasing the number of followers you have, then you are a step closer to obtaining sponsorships for yourself. You may have seen your most loved YouTubers discussing the products or the merchandise they offer through their online stores, and clearly, all the activity gets through their YouTube channels. Not just your merchandise, but you can make use of the same strategy for promoting any affiliate products as well. This is a good strategy for affiliate marketing and selling.

Chapter Ten:
Virtual Assistant

A virtual assistant is essentially a freelancer who provides online assistance by working remotely. You don't have to be physically present at the client's office anymore. You can work from home if you decide to become a virtual assistant. There is a lot of work that needs to be done in any business. However, not all are capable of hiring a person for every task. Most of the startups don't have the finances to hire full-time employees. In such a situation, they outsource a portion of their work to virtual assistants. There are different things that a virtual assistant can and will be required to do. In this chapter, I have categorized all the tasks that a virtual assistant will have to do into seven categories. You can work as a virtual assistant through websites such as fiverr.com and upwork.com.

General or administrative virtual assistants

They are like regular office secretaries. You need to have good time management skills and a good command over the language as well. The usual tasks that you might have to handle would be the emails of your boss and those of the clients, any telephonic inquiries, booking of appointments, managing the appointments, and database management.

Digital marketing virtual assistants

Usually, handles the online marketing campaigns of companies. Digital marketing virtual assistants can be categorized into social media management assistants, SEO assistants and content marketing assistants. The job description usually comprises of analyzing data to achieve the necessary return on investment, planning, scheduling and managing content, making a campaign strategy and analyzing its success, and conducting various analysis as well.

Programming virtual assistants

You will be hired as an assistant developer for a website or a mobile application. Your job profile would include the tasks of designing websites, applications, maintenance and updating the same, debugging and troubleshooting, and uploading new content regularly.

Design virtual assistants

As a design assistant, you will have to make the company's website easy to use and you should possess excellent graphic design skills. You might be required to design the business website, design the mobile application, flyers, business cards, promotional material, product shots, and infographic designs for the same.

Writing virtual assistants

You will be responsible for different types of content writing jobs. You can be a data entry clerk also at times. So, make sure that you are thoroughly enquiring about the position that you are applying for before taking up a job. Usually, you would be required to make plans for content, SEO researching, editing, proofreading, and writing content for SEO.

A/V editing virtual assistants

You will be responsible for all the background tasks that need to be done for editing audio and video. This could mean the removal of clutter, adding sounds for engaging the audience, adding any CGI, providing a sequence to the content given, and making the content audible and visible to the audience.

Financial virtual assistants

A financial virtual assistant would assist in documenting all the financial records, auditing financial statements, analyzing the given information, checking for any discrepancies, advising about money matters, and so on.

No professional degree is necessary to become a virtual assistant, but you should be familiar with the kind of job you are applying for. However, having experience in the area that you applied for will undoubtedly come in handy.

Chapter Eleven:
Freelance Writer/Transcriber

Do you like writing? Do you want to become a professional writer? If yes, then you can do that now! I am not saying that it is easy to become a professional writer, but at some point, you will have to sit down and write some original content. There are different ways in which you can get paid for your writing. Becoming a freelance writer is a great idea! In this chapter, you will learn about different ways in which you can turn your passion and flair for writing into an opportunity to earn money.

Starting a blog

If you want to become a writer, make sure that you have your blog. This will help you in developing a particular writing style as well as an audience for the same. You can advertise about yourself on your blog. Include a "hire me" link in your blog, so that the readers know that you are a writer for hire.

Pitching a guest post

You probably have a couple of blogs that you read daily. Why don't you consider pitching those bloggers to do a guest post on your blog? You can also think about collaborating with other bloggers who share similar interests. This helps in interacting with a broader audience. A lot of blogs also accept guest posts, and they will pay for the same as well. You will have to do a lot of research about this.

Your alma mater

Your alumni magazine probably needs writers, and they would probably love to hire their former students. Read through the guidelines, get acquainted with a few issues, and you can make a pitch for a great idea. Not just that, you can always look for other opportunities at your alma mater like drafting the regular notices and newsletters.

Writing a listicle

Who are the top 10 super villains in the Marvel universe? You are probably coming up with different names in your head. So, why don't you make a note of these names? There are different websites like Listverse or TonTenz that pay for witty and smart top 10 lists. Think about this option if you can come up with quirky ideas.

Self-publishing a book

If you like writing and you want to become an author, you no longer have to find a publisher for yourself. You can publish your book on Amazon or an eBook on Amazon Kindle Direct Publishing. You have to upload your book, get it ready for a kindle, and then start publicizing about it. Don't forget to mention this on your blog. If you aren't sure about finishing a novel, then you can think about serializing it.

Signing up for a content site

You can sign up with a content site and start writing content that you will get paid for. Get familiar with AP writing Style. Learn as much as you can about different styles of writing and make sure that you can follow the brief that a client gives.

Becoming a copywriter

Once you know how to write good content for content sites, you can think about becoming a copywriter as well. You can look at the listings posted on different websites for hiring copywriters, and you can get started with it right away.

Writing fan-fiction

Did you know that Amazon Kindle Worlds is going to pay you to write licensed fan fiction about top-rated television shows? Well, yes! You can certainly cash in on this opportunity. You will need to write 10000+ words on a character you adore, and you will get paid for doing the same.

A good grip on the language and an effortless style of writing are all that you need for becoming a good content writer.

Chapter Twelve:

Amazon FBA

What is FBA?

Fulfillment by Amazon is popularly known as FBA, and it is a third-party logistics service started by Amazon. It helps millions of sellers registered with Amazon across the globe to fulfill their orders. FBA provides you with the option of shipping your old as well as new products to Amazon, instead of shipping them directly to your customers. Once your products reach the Amazon Fulfillment Centers, they will handle the rest. When orders are placed for your products, Amazon will directly pick the stock up from these fulfillment centers and ship them to the customers. They will provide you with shipping facilities, customer service once the order is delivered, and manage customer returns. This will help you save a significant amount of time, effort, and money. Many sellers who have opted for FBA have ended up saving approximately 50% of their shipping costs.

Working with FBA

The working of FBA can be summed up in one sentence "you sell it, we ship it." A private label seller should make the most of Amazon's fulfillment network and their expertise to help in the growth of their business. Your listings on Amazon.com can make use of the free shipping services offered by Amazon, provided the bill amount is above a specified value.

The FBA listings on Amazon.com are listed and then sorted according to the price, and there are no shipping costs involved if the combined value of products is above the value of $35. The FBA listings when accompanied by the FBA logo lets the customers know that the shipping, packing, customer service and all returns are handled solely by Amazon. Using the inventory stored at the Amazon fulfillment center can complete fulfillment of orders, even from other sales channels. The online user interface will let you manage your inventory and at the same time will provide the necessary direction so that the inventory can be returned at any time.

FBA in motion

The following steps explain in brief how the process of FBA works:

Sending products to Amazon

You can send your products, new and used to Amazon's fulfillment center. Seller Central-

Upload the details of your listings. You can decide whether you want Amazon to fulfill either partly or in whole your inventory or not. You can use FBA's Label Service to print labels, or you can also make use of PDF Labels that are provided by Amazon. You can either select your carrier, or you can make use of Amazon's discounted shipping facility.

Receipt and storing of goods by Amazon

As soon as Amazon receives the products, it scans the inventory. The unit dimensions for storage are recorded. Using Amazon's integrated tracking system can monitor your inventory. The products received are cataloged and stored.

Requests for orders

Amazon fulfills the orders placed regardless of whether it has been placed on Amazon.com or any other fulfillment request has been sent for sales, not on Amazon.

Products are picked and packed

Web-to-warehouse, sorting system and high-speed picking system are the technologies adopted by Amazon that let it locate the desired products. Customers have the option of combining products.

Shipping of products

The products are shipped to the customers through the Amazon's fulfillment centers. The products are shipped to the customer depending upon the method selected by them. The required tracking information of the products dispatched is sent to the customers. Customer service can always be contacted for orders that are placed on Amazon.com.

Here are some simple steps that you can follow to add Fulfillment by Amazon to your selling on Amazon Account:

- Go to the Inventory option and click on Manage Inventory.

- To select a product that you want to include in the FBA listing, just click on the box next to it in the left column.

- Now go to Actions and click on Changed to Fulfilled by Amazon.

- And then, all you need to do is follow the directions given to create your first shipment.

Things needed

A Smartphone

A Smartphone is a multidisciplinary tool that finds use in almost all sectors. In the modern age, this tool has proved to be a necessity rather than a luxury. A computer with an active Internet connection is also useful. As your business develops, a Smartphone would be preferred as it gives you a greater sense of flexibility.

A scouting app

A scouting app is handy for a developing business, which can be easily installed on your Smartphone.

A printer

A good quality inkjet color printer with A4 paper sheets (11×17 inches long grain paper)

Packaging equipment

This is the main component of the toolkit. As a seller, you should never run out of these tools. Stack up on your cartons, boxes, labeling sheets, tapes and other stationery that you use for packaging your products.

Chapter Thirteen:
Sell Your Knowledge

Setting up a secondary line of income does sound tempting, doesn't it? However, not everyone has the time to start their own full-fledged business or even freelance. This doesn't mean that there aren't any opportunities for you out there. If you are knowledgeable about a specific area, you can come up with different ways in which you can make use of that knowledge of yours.

E-Book or a white paper

You can transform all the knowledge you possess and the experiences you have had as an investment! You will need to spend considerable time and energy to write an e-book or even publish a white paper, but it will be worth your while. Your vendor will take a cut, but apart from it, you can start selling your work almost immediately! You can write about anything that you are interested in. You can write how-to guides, recipe books, or even papers addressing any of the current issues.

A seminar or a class

Seminars and classes are time-sensitive when compared to other projects that don't require any interaction with others. There are a lot of different ways in which you can make it flexible. One of the most basic things that you will have to do is select a time and date for the class that will work well with your schedule. Once you have done this, you can start planning other details for your class. The primary challenge with this idea is that you will need to be able to convince prospective students to enroll in your class. So, you will need to be able to market your skills well.

Tutoring

If you are good at a particular subject or topic that is taught in school- from kindergarten to grad school- you can consider tutoring. You don't have to worry about any geographical barriers. You can set up your online tutoring program. This will allow you to work with students who are situated in different time zones as well.

Writing for websites

There are plenty of websites that allow writers to write and post numerous articles on their websites. The website is entitled to a percentage of the profits you earn. You can write about anything that interests you, and there are no restrictions regarding any deadlines. You can even stop writing whenever you feel like.

Consulting services

Have you heard of consulting services? Well, with the advent of the Internet, you can offer these services online as well! You can enlist yourself on a website that will help in connecting you with prospective clients who are looking for services that you offer.

Answering questions

Various websites offer payment for answering specific questions. Depending on your areas of interest, you can undoubtedly find a site that you can make use of. If you have good business acumen or a degree in law, you can make use of this to answer specific questions that fall within the purview of your area of expertise.

Chapter Fourteen:
Niche Stores on eBay, Shopify

If you want to become a successful seller, then you should think about niche marketing and selling. You should consider about starting your niche store. A niche is a small part or the sub-market of a more extensive market. Niche stores are usually very competitive, and they have a right demand for the product they are selling.

Find a niche

You will need to find a niche that suits you and the requirements you have in mind. When you do find a niche that you like, type the same into the search bar that's provided on eBay. This will help you in checking the competition that exists. Since you are just getting started with niche selling, make sure that there isn't too much competition. If not, you will have a tough time while selling. Consider different sub-categories of niches as well. Even if it sounds eccentric, it might be lucrative. Do a lot of research and don't just stick to the most obvious options that are available online.

Select a product

You will need to select a product that you want to sell! eBay and Shopify have numerous sellers listed on it. Select products you have a passion for and the work will come easy; you'll enjoy building your shop. Opening up your niche shop can be fun and is an excellent idea if you were always interested in starting your own business.

Your competition

Make it difficult for your competition to offer the same type of products that you are offering. Or make your pricing strategy quite attractive. You should have a unique selling point that will distinguish you from all the other sellers within your niche. Also, make sure that the market is large enough for you to survive.

Setting up your store

You will need to create an eye-catching storefront. There are many ways in which you can personalize your storefront. This personalization is of great importance to ensure that your store stands apart from the rest so that you can grab the attention of potential customers and promote your brand. You can add a banner to your storefront. A banner is a graphic that would run across the page of your store, and you can create this without much difficulty by making use of graphics software and programs like Picasa, Photoshop, and Windows Paint and so on. Always include a shop title and shop announcement. Your shop title would be similar to a tagline, and it would sum up in brief what your shop is all about. Shop announcement is different from a shop title; this would be appearing on the banner, providing information about the products you sell, the materials used and your artistic philosophy if any exists. Your shop announcement can also be made use of to broadcast about any upcoming. There are different types of items that you might sell. If you are selling products like notebooks, magnets, pens, picture frames, then you can organize this as stationery. You can make use of further sections like size, type, material or price as filters when selling these.

Pricing your product

When you start selling your products or goods on your eBay or Shopify store, you might wonder the amount you should charge the customers for your items. If you want to have a profitable online store on these platforms, then you will need to be comfortable going over some numbers and doing a little math regarding your pricing strategy. There are two simple formulae that you will need to learn for this, and they aren't difficult.

The first one is;

(Materials+Labor+Overhead) x2 = Wholesale price

and the second one is;

Wholesale price x2 = Retail price.

But the cost of shipping isn't included in this. The second formula can be adjusted according to your convenience. When you multiply the wholesale price by 2, it will provide the retail price. At times the sellers opt for a number higher than two like 2.5 or 3 to determine their retail price, provided that the market is willing to bear such an expense.

Compose product photos

Products photos that are well photographed can act as a catalyst to promote sales for your eBay store, but you needn't hire a professional photographer to do this. You can very well compose your photos, here are some pointers that will help you portray your product in the best possible manner. All you need is a little bit of artistic flair, some patience, and the following guidelines. You should angle your camera; this means that tilting the camera a little so that it would put the subject matter slightly off center and create some movement and flow. This would produce a picture that is more intriguing. Make sure that you fill the frame with your product so that it not only seems more appealing, but the potential buyers can also see how well-crafted your product is. To highlight your piece dramatically and adding a little bit of panache to it, you can blur the background so that the focus automatically shifts to your product. Always frame your picture with a darker element. You can group your products together, especially if you are into designing or creating itsy bitsy products, then to attract attention, you can group several products together so that the buyer can see how cohesive your products are together. Make use of the rule of thirds. This is a straightforward rule; you will need to divide the scene that you are photographing into nine parts by making use of two horizontal and vertical lines like a tic tac toe grid. This will help in piquing the interest of the viewer.

Compose titles

An item title would be similar to a good headline for a product, and it needs to be designed in such a manner that it would grab the buyer's attention and get them to want to read more about that particular item. You will need to keep it short and contain it to within 155 characters inclusive of spaces. Describe the items at the beginning of the item title so that it would help in improving the chances of searching for a specific item.

Chapter Fifteen:

Direct Sales - What it takes

The process of marketing as well as selling products, in a non-retail setup, directly to the consumer is referred to as direct selling. The sales take place at work, home, or even at a location apart from a store. This system helps in the elimination of middlemen involved in the distribution network. Instead, the products go from the manufacturer to the company taking up direct selling, to the rep or the distributor, and then to the consumer. The products that are sold through direct selling are not usually found in retail outlets. This means that the only way to acquire them is the distributor or the reps. Direct selling isn't the same as direct marketing. In direct marketing, the company bypasses the distributors and other mediators, and instead directly markets to the consumer. Have you ever heard of companies like Silpada or Avon? These are direct selling companies. Direct selling offers you the convenience of working at your hours, earning bonuses, and trips too! You will need to pay a small fee to acquire the starter kit and to make a commission from all the sales you finalize. If you are interested in becoming a successful rep, then here are a couple of things that you should keep in mind.

Company strategy

Some companies will charge you about $10 to buy a starter kit, while for others you might need to stock up on more inventory, and then there are those that have a strict deadline as well. The chances of your success are quite high if your personality and your selling style go hand in hand with the company strategy. So, do some research and talk to a company recruiter about the monthly quota, any incentives, and the selling tools that are necessary.

A product that excites you

You can do your best if you believe in the product that you are selling. If the product that you are selling excites you, it is very likely that the same energy would be transferred to the consumer as well. For instance, if you are a sales rep for a company that deals in clothing and jewelry, then you are the model for the products you are trying to sell! If the thought of maintaining manicured nails for showing off a cocktail ring sounds too time-consuming for you, then this isn't for you. So, select a product that genuinely excites you.

Attitude matters

You must set a couple of realistic goals for yourself regarding what you would like to earn. Like with anything else in life, there will be times when you will feel discouraged. Therefore, you need to set goals for yourself and make sure that the goals are attainable.

Good at networking

Direct selling is all about attracting clients and closing a sale. If you are a social butterfly, then this option might be quite useful! You obviously cannot rely solely on your friends and family members. You should be able to socialize and talk to potential customers at any time and any place without any hesitation.

There are a couple of things that you should keep in mind while you are thinking about making money by taking up direct selling. There are legitimate companies, and then there are those companies that are trying to scam you. Here are a couple of suspicious things that you should watch out for.

The startup cost is high. You have to buy a lot of inventory that cannot be returned. Profits are based on recruiting others, and there isn't any proper information about the company or the firm.

Conclusion

I would like to thank you once again for purchasing my book.

Wouldn't it be wonderful if you could work at your convenience and do things that you genuinely enjoy? You no longer have to sit at a desk and work on something that doesn't interest you. Web businesses are lucrative and exciting. All you need to do is think of an avenue that interests you and get started with your own business! Make use of the information provided in this book to find something that suits your needs. You don't have to stick to just one of the avenues mentioned in this book. You can create multiple streams of income if you want to. Once you have finalized on an idea, the next step is to implement it. All the hard work, effort, and time you put into will be indeed worth it! Take control of your life today and become your own boss!

I really hope you enjoyed this book and it helps you as you begin your exciting journey toward starting your own online business. I would greatly appreciate it if you left my book a review; it really helps indie authors, like myself, out. Thank you so much, my readers truly mean the world to me.

Contact Information:

julie@jrpublishinggroup.com

Website:

www.julierausch.wix.com/author

Please sign up below for my newsletter to receive tips, resources, and **FREEBIES**!

Please click this link for free offer:

"Easy Marketing Tips for Your Home-Based Business"

http://eepurl.com/c8rgw5

www.ingramcontent.com/pod-product-compliance
Lightning Source LLC
Chambersburg PA
CBHW031537210526
45464CB00003B/1056